To parents and teachers

We hope you and the children will enjoy reading this story in either English or Spanish. The story is simple, but not simplified so the language of the Spanish and the English is quite natural but there is lots of repetition.

At the back of the book is a small picture dictionary with the key words and how to pronounce them. There is also a simple pronunciation guide to the whole story on the last page.

Here are a few suggestions on using the book:

- Read the story aloud in English first, to get to know it. Treat it like any other picture book: look at the pictures, talk about the story and the characters and so on.

- Then look at the picture dictionary and say the Spanish names for the key words. Ask the children to repeat them. Concentrate on speaking the words out loud, rather than reading them.

- Go back and read the story again, this time in English and Spanish. Don't worry if your pronunciation isn't quite correct. Just have fun trying it out. Check the guide at the back of the book, if necessary, but you'll soon pick up how to say the Spanish words.

- When you think you and the children are ready, you can try reading the story in Spanish only. Ask the children to say it with you. Only ask them to read it if they are keen to try. The spelling could be confusing and put them off.

- Above all encourage the children to have a go and give lots of praise. Little children are usually quite unselfconscious and this is excellent for building up confidence in a foreign language.

Published by b small publishing
This new edition published in 2018
www.bsmall.co.uk
© b small publishing, 1998, 2018
1 2 3 4 5
All rights reserved. No part of this publication may be reproduced, stored in a retrieval system, or transmitted, in any form or by any means (including electronic, mechanical, photocopying, recording, or otherwise) without prior written permission from the publisher.
Design: Lone Morton and Louise Millar
Editorial: Catherine Bruzzone and Susan Martineau
Production: Madeleine Ehm
Printed in China by WKT Co. Ltd.
ISBN-13: 978-1-911509-71-4
British Library Cataloguing in Publication Data. A catalogue record for this book is available from the British Library.

What's for supper?

¿Qué hay para cenar?

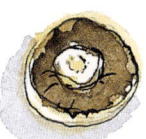

Mary Risk
Pictures by Carol Thompson
Spanish by Rosa Martín

b small publishing
www.bsmall.co.uk

We're cooking the supper tonight, Mum.

Esta noche vamos a preparar la cena *nosotros*, mamá.

It's going to be a surprise.

Va a ser una sorpresa.

Do we need cheese?

¿Necesitamos queso?

Yes, we need cheese, and ham too.

Sí, necesitamos queso y también jamón.

Do we need flour?

¿Necesitamos harina?

Yes.

Sí.

What about potatoes?
Do we need them?

¿Y patatas?
¿Necesitamos patatas?

No, we don't need potatoes.

No, no necesitamos patatas.

But we need tomatoes and mushrooms.

Pero necesitamos tomates y champiñones.

Let's put some olives in it, too!

¡Vamos a ponerle unas aceitunas, también!

Oh no! I don't like olives.

¡Ay no! No me gustan las aceitunas.

How much is all that?

¿Cuánto es todo?

What are you going to make? Please tell me. Please!

No! It's a surprise!

¿Qué vais a hacer?
¡Vamos, decídmelo! ¡Por favor!

¡No! ¡Es una sorpresa!

Here we are home again.

Ya estamos de vuelta en casa.

Don't come into the kitchen, Mum.

No entres en la cocina, mamá.

Supper's ready. It's...

La cena está lista. Es...

Pronouncing French

Don't worry if your pronunciation isn't quite correct. The important thing is to be willing to try. The pronunciation guide here is based on the Spanish accent used in Spain. Although it cannot be completely accurate, it certainly will be a great help:

- Read the guide as naturally as possible, as if it were English.
- Put stress on the letters in *italics*, e.g. ko*thee*na.

If you can, ask a Spanish person to help and move on as soon as possible to speaking the words without the guide.

Note Spanish adjectives usually have two forms, one for masculine and one for feminine nouns. They often look very similar but are pronounced slightly differently, e.g. **listo** and **lista** (see next page).

Words Las palabras
lass pal-*abrass*

to cook supper
preparar la cena
praypah-*rahr* lah *thay*na

tonight
esta noche
*esta noch*eh

surprise
la sorpresa
lah sor*praysa*

cheese
el queso
el *keh*-so

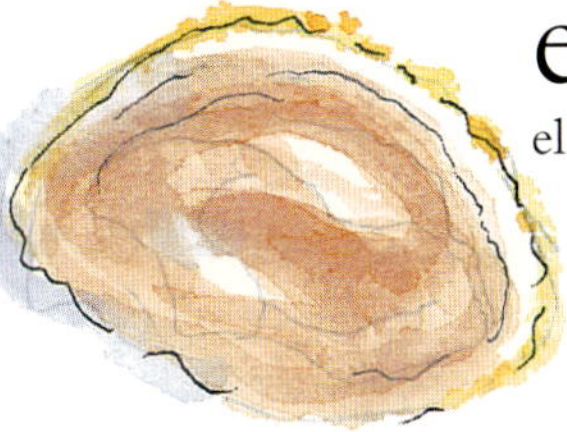

ham
el jamón
el ham*on*

flour
la harina
lah a*reena*

tomato
el tomate
el to*mah*-teh

potato
la patata
lah pa*tah*-ta

olive
la aceituna
lah athay-*too*nah

mushroom
el champiñón
el champeen-*yon*

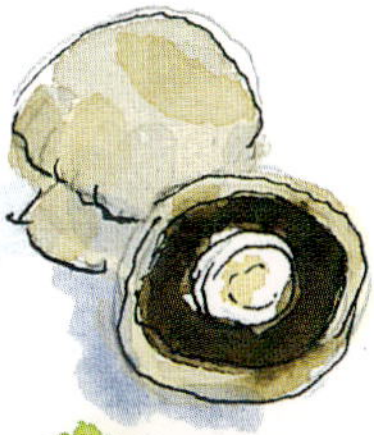

pizza
la pizza
lah *peet*-sah

ready
listo/lista
leesto/leesta

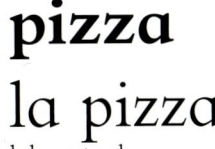

home/house
la casa
lah *kah*-sa

mum
mamá
mam*ma*

dad
papá
*pa*pah

kitchen
la cocina
lah ko*thee*na

yes
sí
see

no
no
noh

please
por favor
poor fa*vor*

A simple guide to pronouncing this French story

¿Qué hay para cenar?
keh aye *par*-ah thay-*nar*

Esta noche vamos a preparar la cena *nosotros*, mamá.
*ess*ta *noch*eh *v*amoss ah praypah-*rahr* lah *thay*na no*ss*otross, mam*m*a

Va a ser una sorpresa.
vah ah sair oona sor*pray*sa

¿Necesitamos queso?
nethessee-*t*amoss *keh*-so

Sí, necesitamos queso y también jamón.
see, nethessee-*t*amoss *keh*-so, ee tamb-*yen* ham*on*

¿Necesitamos harina?.
nethessee-*t*amoss *a*reena

Sí.
see

¿Y patatas?
ee pa*tah*-tass

¿Necesitamos patatas?
nethessee-*t*amoss pa*tah*-tass

No, no necesitamos patatas.
noh, noh nethessee-*t*amoss pa*tah*-tass

Pero necesitamos tomates
pair-ro nethessee-*t*amoss to*mah*-tess

y champiñones.
ee champeen-*yon*ess

¡Vamos a ponerle unas aceitunas también!
*v*amoss ah pon-*air*leh *oo*nas a*th*ay-*too*nass tamb-*yen*

¡Ay no! No me gustan las aceitunas.
aye noh, noh meh *g*oostan lass a*th*ay-*too*nass

¿Cuánto es todo?
k*w*anto ess *toh*-do

¿Qué vais a hacer?
keh vice ah ah-*thair*

¡Vamos, decídmelo! ¡Por favor!
*v*amoss, deh-*theed*-mehlo, poor fav*or*

¡No! ¡Es una sorpresa!
noh, ess *oo*na sor*pray*sa

Ya estamos en la cocina, mamá.
ya esta*m*oss en lah ko*thee*na, mam*m*a

No entres en la cocina, mamá
noh *en*tress en lah ko*thee*na, mam*m*a

La cena está lista. Es...
lah *thay*na ess-*tah lees*ta, ess

¡una pizza!
*oo*na *peet*-sah